Welcome to Your Daily Guide to Living The Way

Inspired by The Way app and Henry Shukman's teachings, this desktop companion offers daily prompts for reflection, grounding, and clarity. Keep it nearby as a steady reminder to live with intention, presence, and an open heart.

In Zen there is a saying: "To begin, begin."

You don't need to prepare for meditation. You don't need to do anything special. You can come exactly as you are. Read a prompt each day, flip through when you need a lift, or share with a friend. Let it be a simple nudge toward a more connected, intentional life.

As the year draws to a close, I want to offer my congratulations on reaching this milestone!

Together, we've explored mindfulness, made space for life's many experiences, and found joy in small, everyday moments.

At its core, mindfulness simply means to notice – our thoughts, our feelings, and this precious life we're living. Wishing you peace and joy ahead. If you'd like to continue the journey, you'll find step-by-step guidance on The Way app.

With love and thanks,

Henry

Scan here to unlock 30 free sessions on The Way app:

Meet Henry Shukman. Henry is a respected meditation teacher and Zen Master known for making ancient Zen wisdom accessible today. As Spiritual Director Emeritus of Mountain Cloud Zen Center and co-founder of The Way app, he blends deep spiritual insight with everyday mindfulness. His memoir *One Blade of Grass* shares how Zen helped him heal from personal trauma and find peace. Through teaching and writing, Shukman guides others toward clarity, connection, and awakening through meditation.

Scan here to unlock 30 free sessions on The Way app:

What is this (part ii)

As we did on our very first day this year, just notice how you're feeling in this moment, as you read these words. What emotions are coming up? Remember, there's no 'perfect way' that we should be feeling. Every experience is welcome. Now and for always.

Welcome to The Way

Welcome to this journey of meditation. For today, just notice how you're feeling in this moment, as you read these words. Rushed? Excited? Tired? Anxious? There's no 'perfect way' that we ought to be feeling. Every experience is welcome.

What is this (part i)

Approach today as a perpetual beginner.
No matter how much you know, there's
always more to discover. How humbling –
and how exciting.

What is The Way?

Bring your attention to your jaw. Can you release it by letting it lower just a little bit? We often carry unnoticed tension there. What does it feel like to let your jaw go slack, just for a moment?

FACES OF FLOW

Now

Each morning is a blank page waiting for your story. What beautiful things will you write with your actions today?

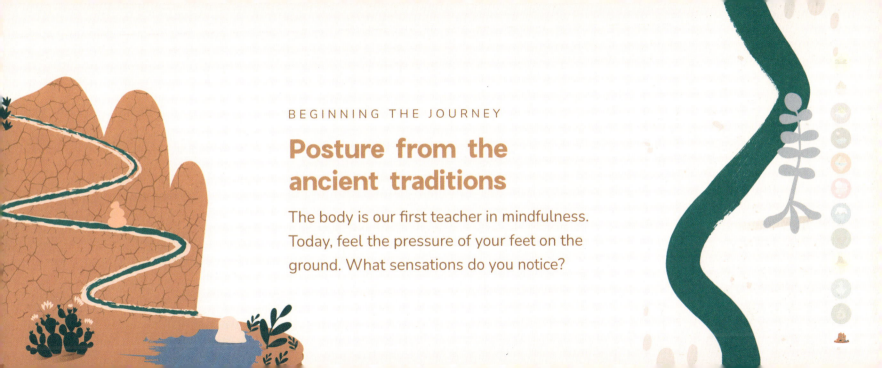

BEGINNING THE JOURNEY

Posture from the ancient traditions

The body is our first teacher in mindfulness. Today, feel the pressure of your feet on the ground. What sensations do you notice?

New

See every interaction as a teacher today. The person who frustrates you, the unexpected delay – what are they here to show you?

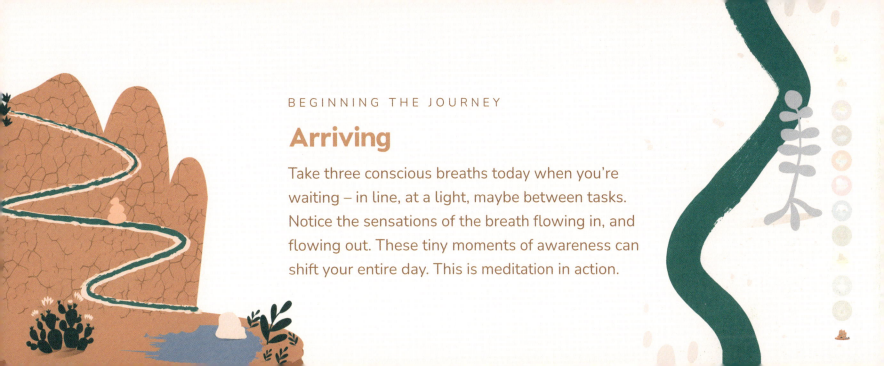

Arriving

Take three conscious breaths today when you're waiting – in line, at a light, maybe between tasks. Notice the sensations of the breath flowing in, and flowing out. These tiny moments of awareness can shift your entire day. This is meditation in action.

FACES OF FLOW

Beginner's mind

Feel your natural dignity today. Not from achievement or status, but from being part of life itself. You belong here exactly as you are.

A word from Henry

Your heart has carried you through every moment of your life, beating steadily whether you noticed it or not. Place a gentle hand on your chest. Feel its rhythm. This is the pulse of life itself moving through you. What a gift to be alive.

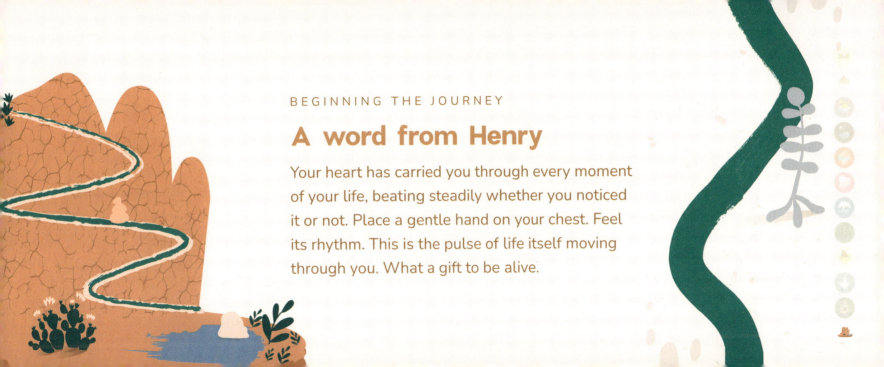

Beauty and flow

Think of a time when you felt true joy. Let yourself remember this moment with fondness, and allow it to bring a smile to your face. Where were you? Who were you with? How did it feel? Let this memory be a reminder of the beauty that each day holds. You are always creating your next memory.

Journey into the unknown

If difficulties arise today, try this: Stop for a moment. Feel your feet on the ground. Notice the space around your body. Remember that challenges come and go like weather, while your awareness remains like the vast, open sky.

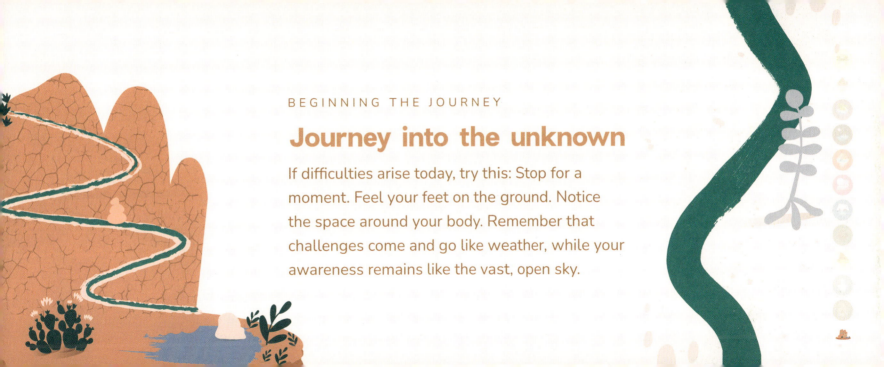

FACES OF FLOW

Go straight on

Notice what gives and takes energy today.
Some activities nourish, others drain. What
are some ways you can fill your cup today?
Can you share this with others?

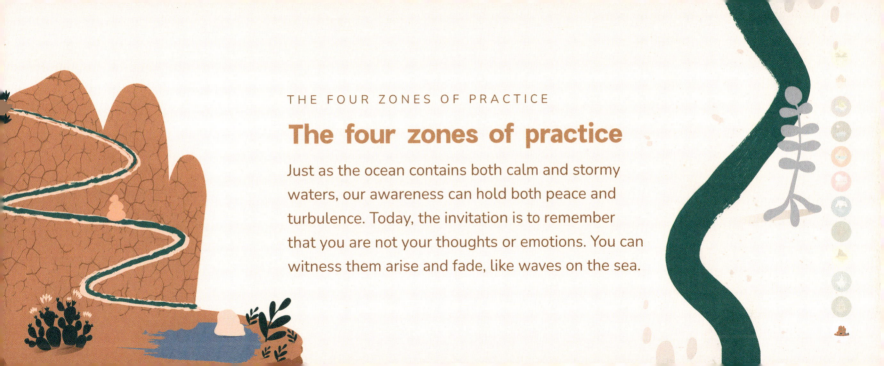

The four zones of practice

Just as the ocean contains both calm and stormy waters, our awareness can hold both peace and turbulence. Today, the invitation is to remember that you are not your thoughts or emotions. You can witness them arise and fade, like waves on the sea.

Letting it all go

Think back to when you played as a child.
When you danced, played, and sang with
pure innocence and wonder. No expectations,
no judgements. Can you let yourself feel that
childlike joy again? What would happen if
you let it all go?

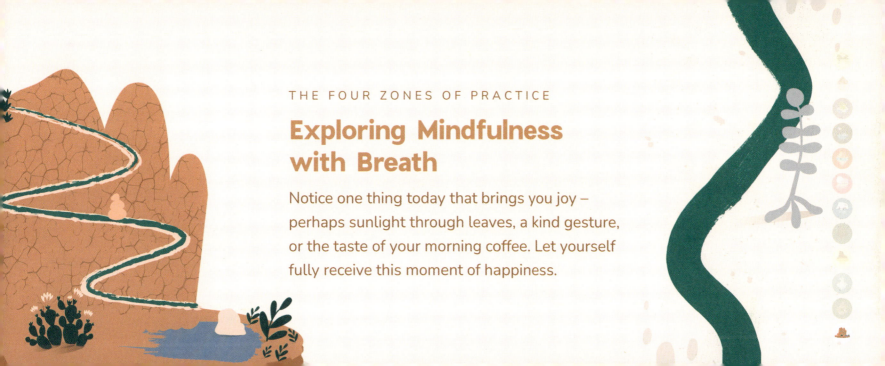

THE FOUR ZONES OF PRACTICE

Exploring Mindfulness with Breath

Notice one thing today that brings you joy — perhaps sunlight through leaves, a kind gesture, or the taste of your morning coffee. Let yourself fully receive this moment of happiness.

This

Listen to the symphony of sounds around you today. Traffic, birds, voices, wind – all instruments in life's orchestra. No need to judge, just appreciate.

Exploring Support with Breath

The breath you're taking right now connects you to all living beings. Every creature that has ever lived has breathed this same air.

Just this

Life lives itself through all beings. The same force that grows trees flows through you. You belong to this one living world.

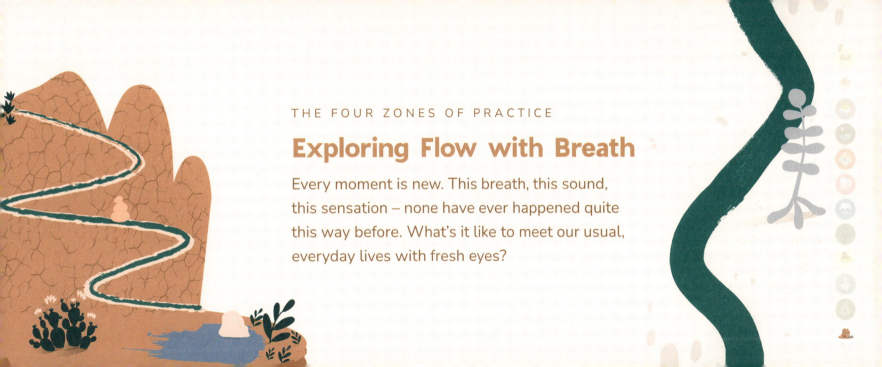

Exploring Flow with Breath

Every moment is new. This breath, this sound, this sensation – none have ever happened quite this way before. What's it like to meet our usual, everyday lives with fresh eyes?

FACES OF FLOW

It's just like this

Mountains don't compare themselves to other mountains. They simply rise in their own magnificent way. Be beautifully, uniquely you today.

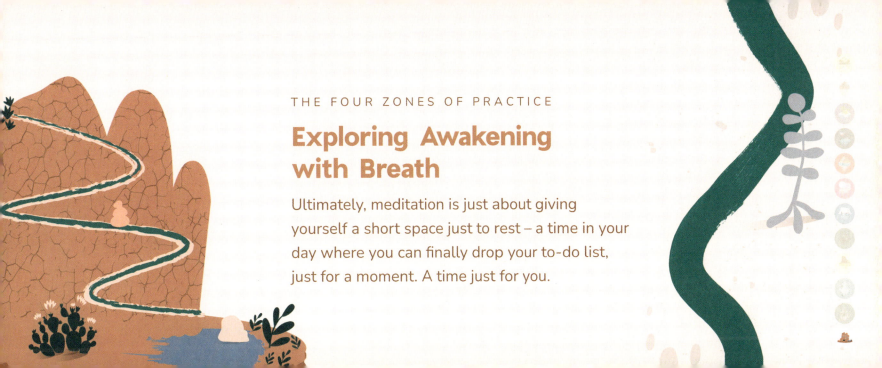

THE FOUR ZONES OF PRACTICE

Exploring Awakening with Breath

Ultimately, meditation is just about giving yourself a short space just to rest – a time in your day where you can finally drop your to-do list, just for a moment. A time just for you.

Introduction to Deeper Flow

Take a moment today to notice how far you've come. Like a tree adding rings year by year, you're constantly growing. But often we don't notice if we don't stop and look.

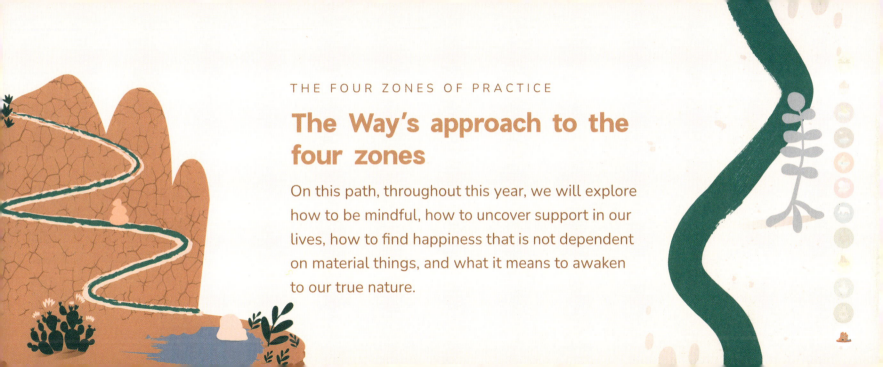

THE FOUR ZONES OF PRACTICE

The Way's approach to the four zones

On this path, throughout this year, we will explore how to be mindful, how to uncover support in our lives, how to find happiness that is not dependent on material things, and what it means to awaken to our true nature.

INTER-BEING

Inter-being

Every star plays its part in lighting the night sky. Your presence matters more than you know.

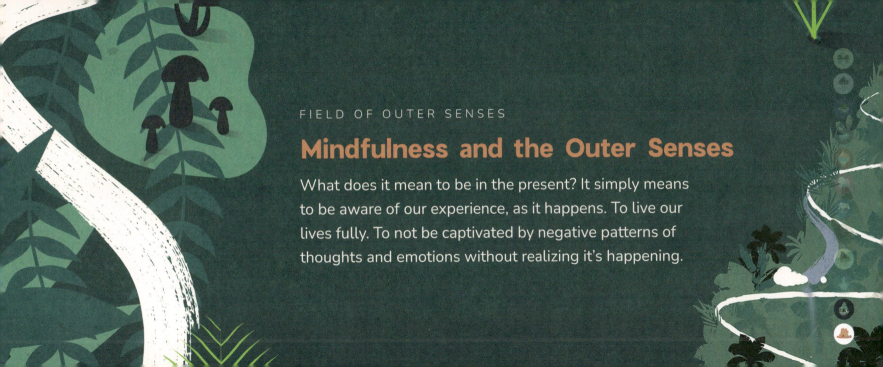

Mindfulness and the Outer Senses

What does it mean to be in the present? It simply means to be aware of our experience, as it happens. To live our lives fully. To not be captivated by negative patterns of thoughts and emotions without realizing it's happening.

INTER-BEING

Sharing feelings

Before responding to situations today, check in with your heart. Beyond thoughts and reactions lies a deeper wisdom, practice allowing that wisdom to be your guide.

Scanning the body

Being aware of the body is the simplest way to come back to the present. Can you notice the sensation in your feet or hands, right now? That is being present!

INTER-BEING

Shared heart-mind

Hold your opinions lightly today. Practice curiosity instead of certainty. What might you discover if you don't already know?

FIELD OF OUTER SENSES

Sensing the whole body

The body knows how to bring you home to presence.
Let it guide you. Try noticing how your body is feeling.

INTER-BEING

A single web of inter-being

Let kindness be your quiet revolution today. Not as a duty, but as a natural expression of your true nature. Small acts can transform the world.

FIELD OF OUTER SENSES

Working with labels for the body

Happiness often arrives in small moments – a warm shower, morning light, a friend's smile. Today, let yourself fully receive these simple gifts.

INTER-BEING

Body and ancestry

Look at a tree or plant today. Notice how it simply grows where it's planted, flourishing in its own way. You too can thrive exactly where you are.

Working with labels for hearing

When difficulties arise today, remember – you are larger than any single experience. Like the sky holding all weather, you can hold all that arises.

INTER-BEING

Body and biosphere

Create small spaces of kindness today. A moment to check on someone, a pause to appreciate beauty, a breath to reset. These tiny gaps let love flow.

The soundscape

Today, try to pause occasionally to listen. Not to anything specific – just open your ears to the soundscape around you. Notice how this brings you immediately into the present.

INTER-BEING

Air

Feel gratitude for your body's countless processes today — breathing, digesting, healing — all happening without your conscious control. You're supported by life itself.

The field of sight

We are surrounded by beauty, often without ever seeing it. Try this: with eyes closed, notice the subtle play of light and shadow, behind your eyelids. There's always something to see, even in darkness.

Introduction to inter-being

The summit remembers not how fast you climbed, but that you kept going. Today, celebrate each step forward, no matter how small.

FIELD OF OUTER SENSES

An experience in the desert

You're breathing right now — with no effort required. The body knows exactly what to do. Can you trust this natural wisdom that keeps you alive?

INTER-CONNECTING

All beings

When someone seems difficult today, remember they too have struggles you can't see. Let this understanding naturally soften your response.

Training two senses: Body and seeing

Notice any tension you're holding as you read this. Shoulders, jaw, belly. There is no need to change anything – just bringing gentle attention often allows things to release naturally.

Sympathetic joy

We hold so many contrasts in our day to day, but we struggle when we encounter contrasts to our ego. How can our system handle heat and cold, blood and oxygen, pathogens and antibodies, but we cannot handle a different perspective? Try to embrace the power of holding two ideas together.

Training two senses: Body and hearing

The simple act of naming what is present in our experience draws us deeper into the present and lets us actually see the richness of our lives.

Compassion (part iii)

When you see suffering today, don't turn away. Let your natural compassion arise without forcing it. Your heart knows how to respond.

Training two senses: Seeing and hearing

We're always looking out at the field of sight in front of us. But do we ever stop to consider what it is we're actually looking at?

INTER-CONNECTING

Compassion (part ii)

Notice the invisible threads connecting you to others today – shared smiles, common hopes, mutual support. We're all in this together.

All three outer senses together

By coming back to the present moment, we allow ourselves to rest our nervous systems and to appreciate the very fact of being alive.

INTER-CONNECTING

Heart knowledge

Trust what your heart knows. Beyond
thoughts and logic lies a deeper wisdom.
Let it guide your choices.

Introducing the inner system

Just as the outer world has sights and sounds, your inner world has thoughts and feelings. Can you take a moment to notice this inner landscape, right now? What thoughts and feelings are arising?

INTER-CONNECTING

Compassion (part i)

Think of how birds sing not to be heard, but because it's their nature. Your authentic joy gives others permission to shine too.

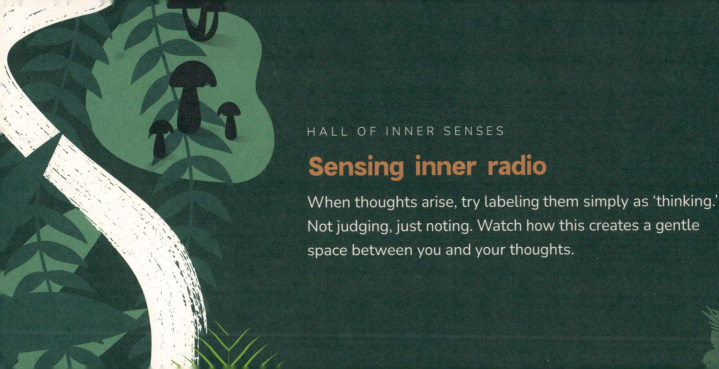

Sensing inner radio

When thoughts arise, try labeling them simply as 'thinking.'
Not judging, just noting. Watch how this creates a gentle
space between you and your thoughts.

INTER-CONNECTING

Kindness (part ii)

Sync with nature's pace today. Notice dawn and dusk, meal times, rest times. Let your body's wisdom align with Earth's natural cycles.

Sensing inner video

See if you can notice your mind's eye – the place where images are projected in the mind. What do you see?

INTER-CONNECTING

Kindness (part i)

Feel your partnership with life today. Each breath is a collaboration with plants, your body an orchestra of cooperation. You belong here completely.

Training two senses: Radio and video

Your mind naturally produces thoughts, like your body produces sensations. Today, can you let thoughts come and go like clouds in the sky?

INTER-CONNECTING

Self-caring

The morning dew makes every leaf sparkle. Today, notice the small moments that make your life shine. How can you share this sparkle today?

Sensing emotion

Happiness isn't about having no thoughts, but about finding peace with the thinking mind. Don't try to push away thoughts. Just notice them as they come and go.

INTER-CONNECTING

Basic goodness

Beneath our differences, all humans share the same basic hopes and fears. Today, let this understanding guide your interactions.

Training three senses: All inner senses

Every thought is temporary, like ripples on water. Today, watch how thoughts naturally arise and dissolve when not held onto.

Inter-connection

Like wind carrying seeds to new gardens, your words of encouragement might travel further than you know. Plant something beautiful today.

Bringing it together: all Outer and Inner senses

Your heart area holds emotional wisdom. Today, place a gentle hand on your chest and feel what's present. No need to analyze, just be with what's here.

GUESTHOUSE

Refuge

Create a gentle evening routine. Maybe a warm drink, some light stretching, or a few minutes of quiet breathing. Give your system a chance to naturally unwind.

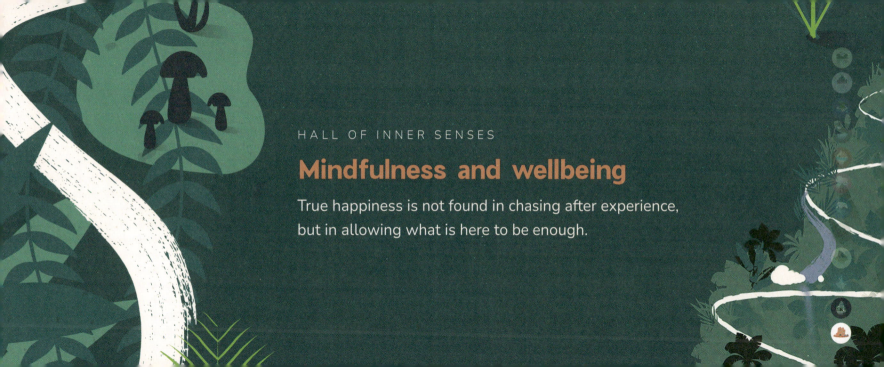

HALL OF INNER SENSES

Mindfulness and wellbeing

True happiness is not found in chasing after experience,
but in allowing what is here to be enough.

GUESTHOUSE

Ancestors

Your body carries the wisdom of countless ancestors. Today, notice how your instincts and emotions connect you to all who came before. Do you see how everything supports everything else? The sun grows food, rain fills rivers, others' work makes your life possible. We are all part of one system.

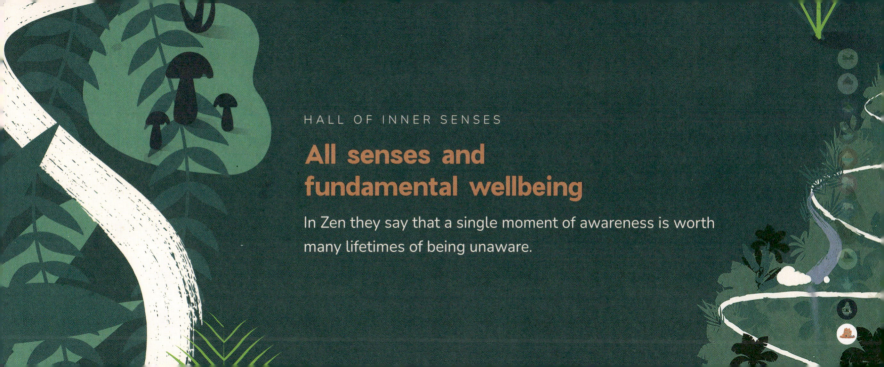

All senses and fundamental wellbeing

In Zen they say that a single moment of awareness is worth many lifetimes of being unaware.

Guesthouse (part ii)

Feel yourself as part of Earth's living system today. Your body is made of star-stuff and soil, water and air. Let this understanding expand your sense of self.

Introducing the Hindrances

Challenges will always come up for us in life. The only question is – how will we choose to meet them?

The truth of impermanence

The air you breathe has traveled the world. Today, remember how each breath connects you to all life – the same air moves through all beings.

The first hindrance: Restlessness

When difficulties arise, we usually try to push them away. What if there was a way to let them be a natural part of our experience?

GUESTHOUSE

Home

Like how a mirror can catch a glint of the sun
when tilted in the right position, you can be
the reason someone shines their light with the
world. Your energy can transform everything
for another person. Share that energy and be
the reason someone shines today.

The second hindrance: Reluctance

Anxiety is not a flaw, but a natural part of being human.
If it arises, try to meet it with patience and kindness.

GUESTHOUSE

Homecoming

The sun doesn't question its light – it simply shines. Today, trust that you too have gifts meant for sharing.

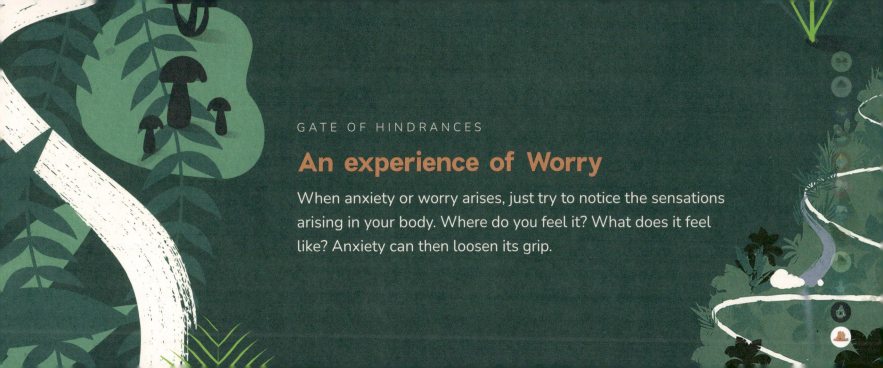

An experience of Worry

When anxiety or worry arises, just try to notice the sensations arising in your body. Where do you feel it? What does it feel like? Anxiety can then loosen its grip.

Impermanence

Remember that everything we experience is changing. We all encounter pain, sorrow, heartache, sadness – but they pass.
Think about the last time you got through something difficult – how did you overcome it? Everything is impermanent.

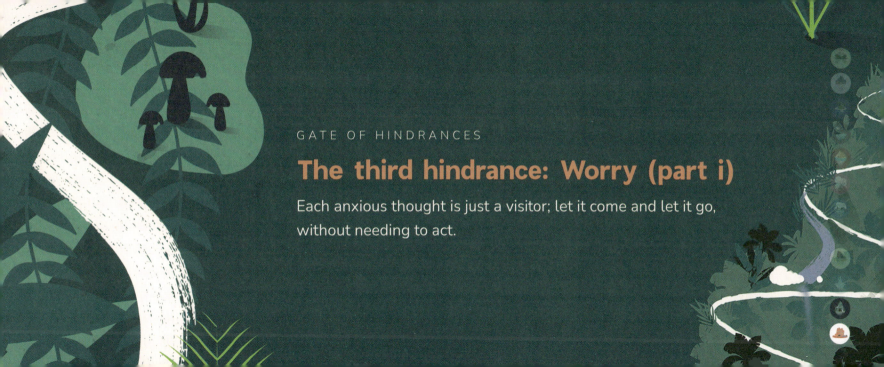

The third hindrance: Worry (part i)

Each anxious thought is just a visitor; let it come and let it go, without needing to act.

Guesthouse (part i)

Approach one challenging situation today with curiosity instead of judgment. What might you learn? Let wonder replace worry.

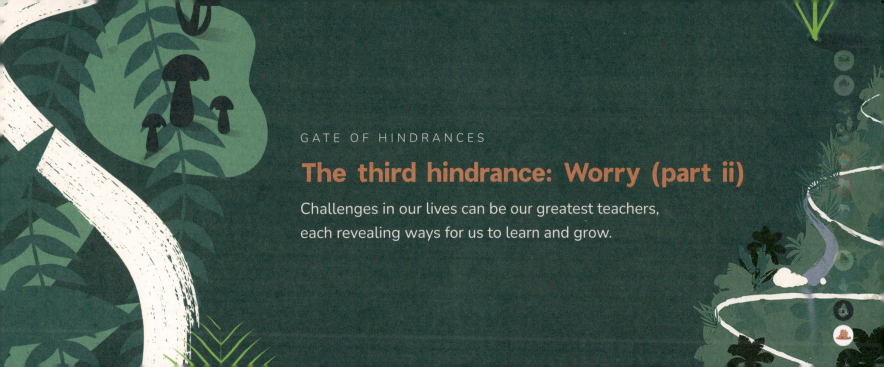

GATE OF HINDRANCES

The third hindrance: Worry (part ii)

Challenges in our lives can be our greatest teachers,
each revealing ways for us to learn and grow.

GUESTHOUSE

Exploring
the guesthouse

Choose one small area to organize today. A
clear space helps create a clear mind. Let the
simple act of tidying become a meditation.

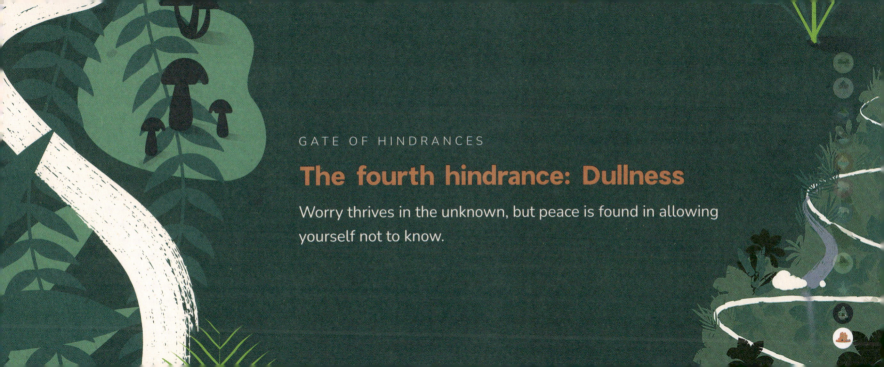

The fourth hindrance: Dullness

Worry thrives in the unknown, but peace is found in allowing yourself not to know.

THRESHOLD

From far

Engage your senses fully in one everyday
activity — feeling warm water while washing
dishes, smelling fresh laundry, really
listening to the sounds of the household.

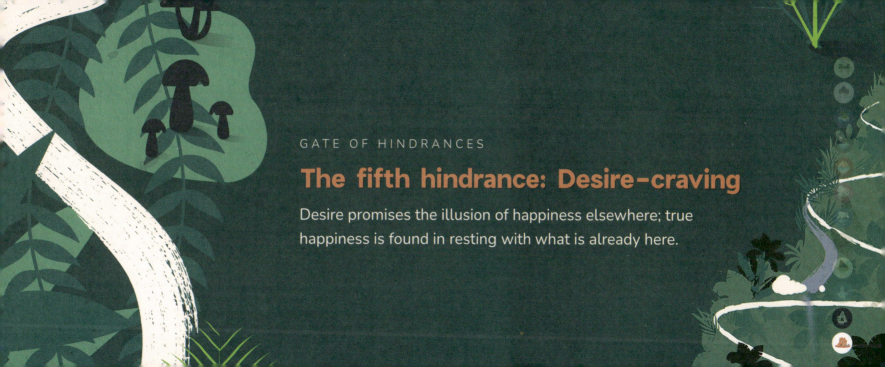

The fifth hindrance: Desire-craving

Desire promises the illusion of happiness elsewhere; true happiness is found in resting with what is already here.

THRESHOLD

Boundary

Set healthy boundaries with technology today. Maybe no phone during meals, or a device-free hour before bed. Notice how this affects your peace.

GATE OF HINDRANCES

The sixth hindrance: Aversion-resistance

Rest is the antidote to worry; let all systems power down and discover the quiet underneath.

THRESHOLD

It doesn't matter

Practice giving others the gift of space today. Listen without fixing, accept without judging. Notice how this spaciousness nurtures relationships.

The seventh hindrance: Doubt

Doubt is the mist that obscures the path; patience and presence are the morning sun that clears it.

THRESHOLD

The Earth was all before me

Find pockets of silence in your day – before others wake, in your car, between tasks. Let quiet moments restore your energy.

Just being still

Awareness is the space that holds all our experience, without preference.

The quiet

Whatever the weather – internal or external – practice acceptance today. Let difficult moments be like passing clouds. Nothing to fix, just experience.

Coming home

Stillness is a radical act in a hectic world. What is it like to be still, just for a moment, in the midst of a busy day?

THRESHOLD

Joy through others

Practice celebrating others' success today. When someone shares good news, let your happiness for them be genuine. Their joy can multiply your own.

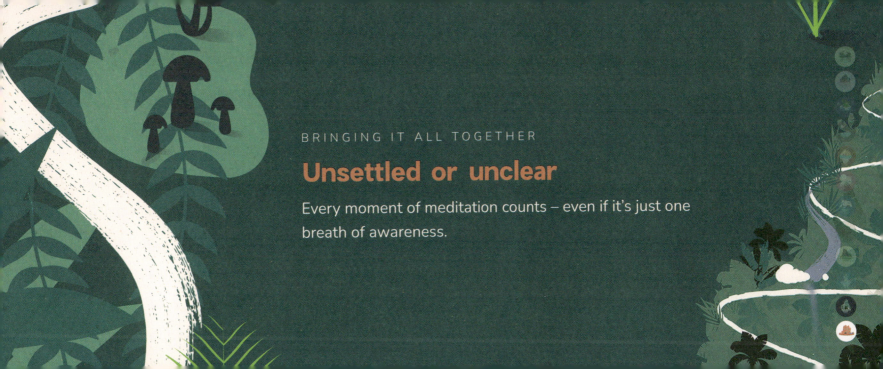

Unsettled or unclear

Every moment of meditation counts – even if it's just one breath of awareness.

Life as a guesthouse

Listen to your inner voice today. Is it harsh or kind? Practice speaking to yourself as you would a dear friend. Let your inner dialogue nurture growth.

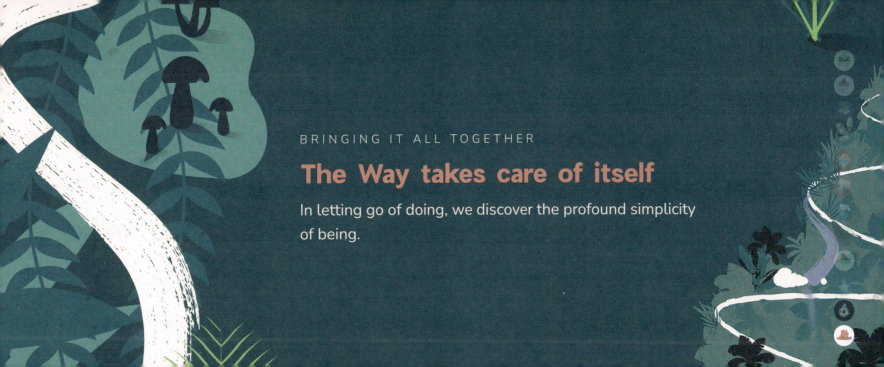

BRINGING IT ALL TOGETHER

The Way takes care of itself

In letting go of doing, we discover the profound simplicity of being.

THRESHOLD

Caravan

When you meet someone struggling today, pause and think: "Just like me, they want to be happy." Let this understanding naturally soften your heart.

Building blocks

Where do thoughts come from? Where do they go to?
Can you track the journey of a thought, from when it
enters your mind to when it leaves it?

THRESHOLD

You're not alone

Listen to what you need today. Sometimes self-care means just giving your body and nervous system the chance for a brief rest. A short respite from the constant daily demands we make on ourselves.

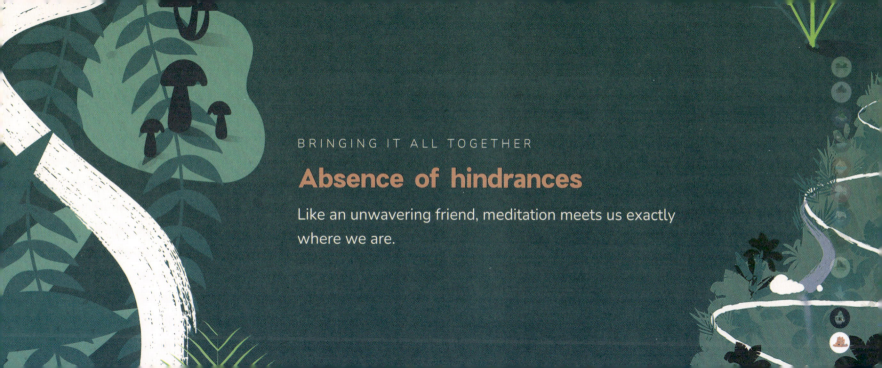

BRINGING IT ALL TOGETHER

Absence of hindrances

Like an unwavering friend, meditation meets us exactly
where we are.

Open and gone

Feel the basic goodness of your heart today.
Beneath all thoughts and emotions lies a
fundamental warmth and wisdom. Trust this.

Just sitting

The only thing we truly have is now — let awareness make it enough. If we spend too much time in the past or the future, we lose this present moment.

Open to all (part ii)

Wherever you are today, practice being at home in this moment. Your true home isn't a place – it's the peace of being fully present.

OCEAN OF BREATH

Introduction to Support

Day to day, moment to moment, we are supported by a multitude of small causes and effects that we barely ever notice. But with a little bit of patience and attention, we can begin to uncover them.

Open awareness

Notice how everything is always changing. Today, rather than resisting change, practice saying "yes" to life's natural flow. Change is how we grow.

OCEAN OF BREATH

Spacious breath

Take a moment to breathe deeply and slowly.
Feel your chest and belly filling. Notice how it
feels to breathe.

Open to all (part i)

Step back today and see your life from afar. Small problems often fade when seen from a distance. What really matters from this wider view?

OCEAN OF BREATH

Breath as support

Every breath you take keeps you alive, moment to moment. It gives you new life. It's a precious gift, and one given freely.

OPEN AWARENESS

Passenger

You're a passenger on life's great journey. Today, practice relaxing into the ride rather than trying to control it. Let life carry you.

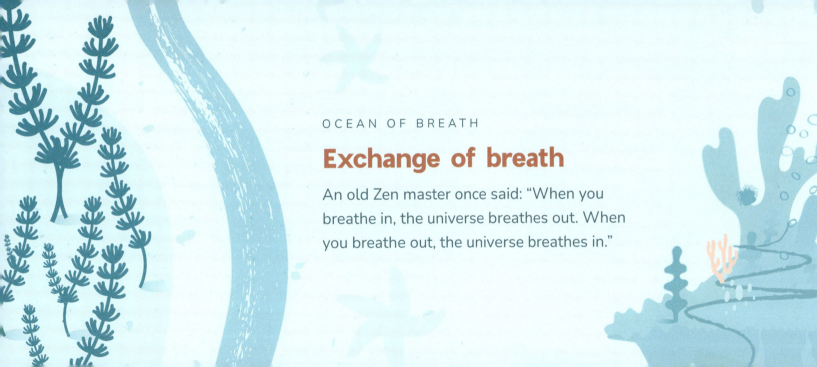

OCEAN OF BREATH

Exchange of breath

An old Zen master once said: "When you breathe in, the universe breathes out. When you breathe out, the universe breathes in."

OPEN AWARENESS

Out and in

Notice the simple space around you right now – the room you're in, the air you're breathing. Your awareness just naturally holds all of today's experiences.

OCEAN OF BREATH

A single word from a stranger

Each breath is a doorway back to peace – and is always there waiting for us. Try noticing your breath at least three times today.

Just out

Look at the world today as if you've never seen it before. What's here, fresh and new, before your stories about it? Let each moment surprise you.

OCEAN OF BREATH

Carried by breath

Help can arrive from where we least expect it.
All we need to do is be open to it showing up.

OPEN AWARENESS

Just seeing

In the midst of noise and activity today, remember the quiet at your core. Like a deep ocean beneath surface waves, peace is always available.

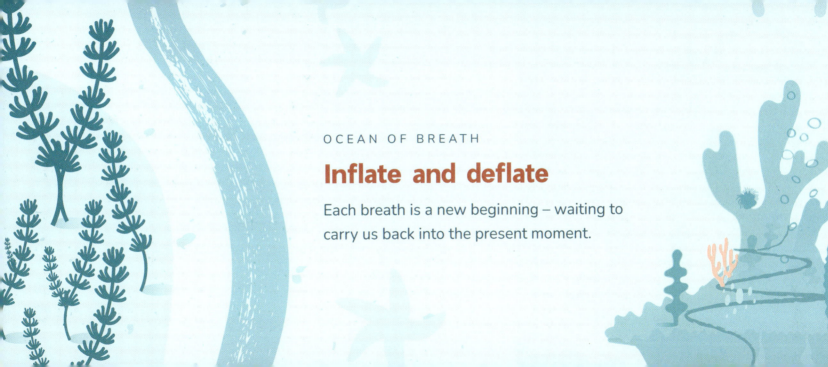

OCEAN OF BREATH

Inflate and deflate

Each breath is a new beginning – waiting to carry us back into the present moment.

OPEN AWARENESS

One awareness with eyes open

Think of a forest – some trees reach for light while others thrive in shade, yet all belong. Today, let your mind be as spacious as these woods.

FOUNDATION OF FOUR ELEMENTS

Introducing the Four Elements

Without air we suffocate in minutes. Without heat we perish in hours. Without water we expire in days. Without food from the earth we starve in weeks. But how often do we really notice these things keeping us alive?

OPEN AWARENESS

Outer experience with eyes open

Extend your circle of care today. Beyond family and friends, include strangers, animals, plants. Notice how your heart naturally expands.

FOUNDATION OF FOUR ELEMENTS

The earth's support

Can you notice that you are supported, right now, by the earth underneath your feet?

OPEN AWARENESS

Open eyes and open awareness

Think of how we view old trees – their twisted branches and weathered bark only add to their beauty. Can you see your own life story with this same appreciation?

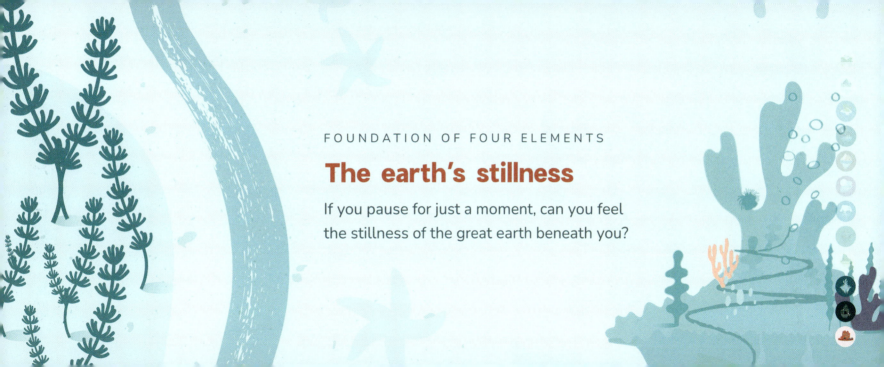

FOUNDATION OF FOUR ELEMENTS

The earth's stillness

If you pause for just a moment, can you feel
the stillness of the great earth beneath you?

Resting in both

Today, practice just being here. No need to achieve anything or get anywhere. Like a mountain simply being a mountain, let yourself simply be.

FOUNDATION OF FOUR ELEMENTS

The earth's substance

We are made of the very same stuff – the chemistry, the molecules, the matter – as this earth itself.

Underlying awareness

Notice who's seeing when you look around today. Is there a separate "you" watching, or is seeing happening by itself? Let this question open your experience.

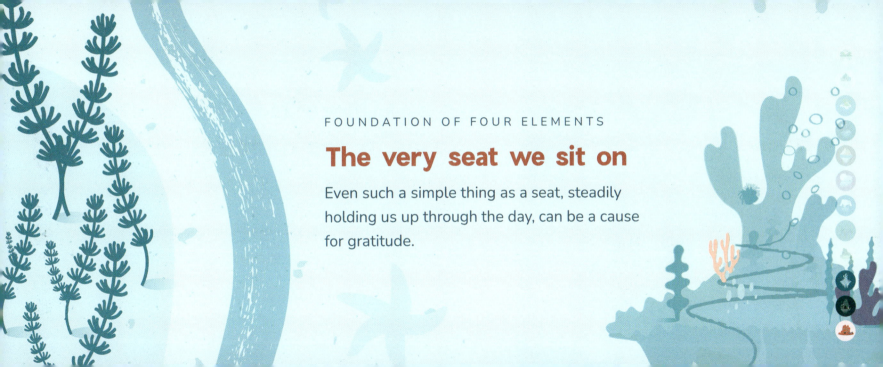

FOUNDATION OF FOUR ELEMENTS

The very seat we sit on

Even such a simple thing as a seat, steadily holding us up through the day, can be a cause for gratitude.

Space in the middle

With eyes open, practice staying present today. Let your gaze be soft, receiving the world without analyzing. Everything can be meditation.

FOUNDATION OF FOUR ELEMENTS

Opening to warmth (part i)

What a beautiful thing it is to feel warm enough. To be warmed by the sun, by clothes, by our homes.

The power of labelling

Music comes alive in the dance between sound and silence. Today, appreciate how different voices – even those that challenge you – create life's fuller symphony.

Opening to warmth (part ii)

Can you tune into the sensation of warmth, right now? How does it feel to be a warm and nourished body?

Resting with inner and outer

Look back at who you were five years ago. Notice the wisdom you've gained, the strength you've developed. Every experience has shaped you. Where will you be 5 years from now? You will still be you.

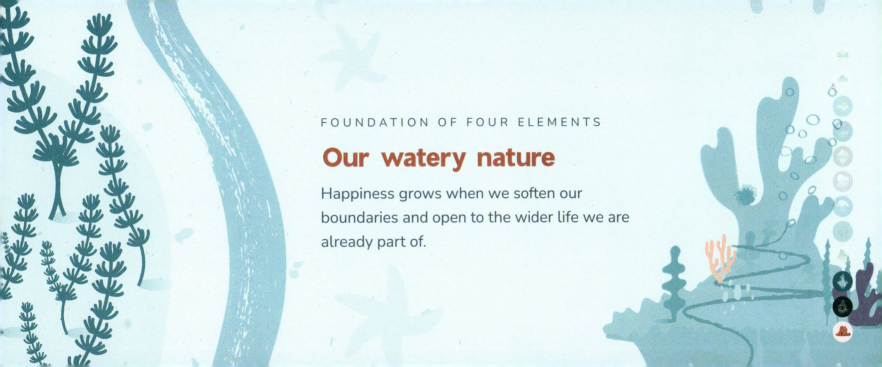

FOUNDATION OF FOUR ELEMENTS

Our watery nature

Happiness grows when we soften our boundaries and open to the wider life we are already part of.

Inner and outer

When we name experiences in our minds, it can change them. Today, try holding your experience lightly, before labels. What's here before you label it "good" or "bad" in your mind?

GIFT OF MIND AND HEART

Gift of mind and heart

Without awareness, without consciousness, without our human minds – we would not get to experience life at all. What an incomparable gift we are given.

Inner experience

Stand before a garden and notice what catches your eye – the blooming flowers or the few scattered weeds? Today, try seeing yourself with this same generous gaze, focusing on what's flowering within you.

GIFT OF MIND AND HEART

Human consciousness

This scarred and patched-up old wineskin of a
heart – a heart that every human being has –
what a thing it is!

Outer experience

When meeting others today, silently
acknowledge their fundamental goodness.
Let your heart recognize their heart.

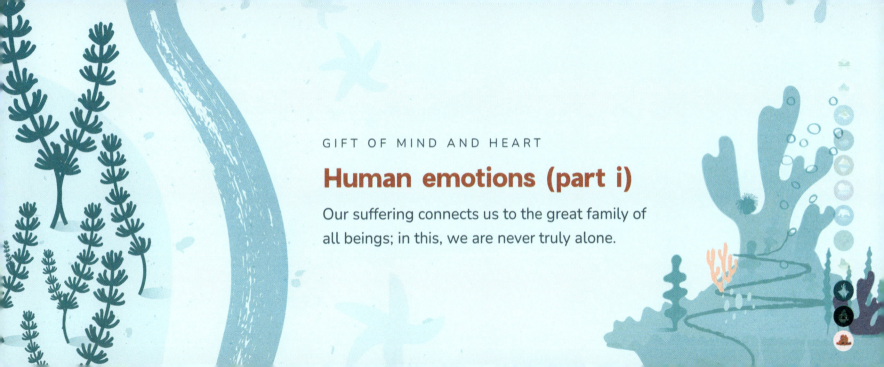

GIFT OF MIND AND HEART

Human emotions (part i)

Our suffering connects us to the great family of all beings; in this, we are never truly alone.

Coming back to inner and outer experience

Practice this: In your mind's eye, imagine a place that brings you peace and happiness. Think about this for a few moments. What does it look like? Who is with you? How does it feel? Imagine this place without attachment; nothing to hold, nothing to push away.

Human emotions (part ii)

What a gift it is to be able to experience comfort, joy, and love.

Lake of awareness (part ii)

The simple act of pausing and bringing a small smile to your face can change our inner world, just for a moment.

GIFT OF MIND AND HEART

Shared consciousness with a mentor

It is said that wisdom and compassion are the two wings of practice. What ways can you find to bring a little more compassion into your day, today?

Heart and body

Let your body inform you today. Notice where you hold tension, where you feel ease. Your body always knows what's true – listen to its wisdom.

GIFT OF MIND AND HEART

Whose mind is this?

One promise of meditation is that in time,
our awareness can become infused with
compassion, both for ourselves and for others.

Guesthouse

Your experience is like a guesthouse. Today, welcome each thought and feeling as an honored guest. Even difficult visitors might bring unexpected gifts.

GIFT OF MIND AND HEART

Shared compassion

Meditation is not about becoming something,
but about realizing what you already are.

Lake of awareness (part i)

Imagine your awareness as a deep, calm lake. Let all experiences – thoughts, emotions, sensations – float on its surface while the depths remain serene.

Introduction to Flow

One fundamental part of our human nature is flow states. Moments of deep fulfillment that happen when we are absorbed in a task. Meditation can help us explore these and help us to access them more regularly.

Recognizing emotions

Practice naming emotions as they arise today: "Ah, anxiety is here," "Now excitement," "Here's frustration." Naming with gentleness helps create space around feelings.

FOREST OF EASE

Release in the body

Just for a moment, as you read this, let your breath be like ocean waves — no forcing, no controlling. Just watching its natural rhythm. Notice how this watching itself brings ease.

Inner kindness

When difficult feelings arise today, place a hand on your heart and say silently: "May I be kind to myself in this moment." Let self-compassion be your first response.

Release in the mind

Practice this: pause for a moment and bring a half-smile on your face. We're not meditating, we're just resting. How does it feel?

HEART AREA

Allowing feelings

Whatever emotion visits today, give it permission to be here. Happy, sad, angry, afraid – all are welcome guests in your heart's guesthouse.

FOREST OF EASE

Release in the heart

Sometimes meditation flows by itself, like a river carrying you. Today, see if you can notice any moments when effort just falls away and the moment takes over.

Exploring the heart area

Like a meteorologist, we can track our emotional weather. Notice feelings arise and pass without trying to change them. You're the sky; emotions are just weather.

FOREST OF EASE

Release in the moment

Like the moon reflecting in water, flow states show themselves when the mind becomes still. Can you take a moment as you read this to let your body and mind fall still?

Peace in the heart area

Place a hand on your heart today when you need comfort. Feel its steady rhythm. This simple gesture can bring peace amid any storm. You carry this sanctuary within you always.

FOREST OF EASE

Carried by ease

The practice for today: just for a moment
let your attention be soft and wide. Let your
gaze soften. Let things be as they are. There's
no need to change anything.

Introduction to the heart area

Start your day with intention. Before rushing into your to-do list and all the activities of the day, take three minutes to feel your breath and set a simple aim for the day.

No effort

If you ever find yourself trying too hard to achieve a certain outcome, remember: sometimes things come from letting go, not from grasping.

Origin of thought

The path you're walking today may become someone else's guiding light tomorrow. Each step through difficulty leaves a trail of courage that others can follow.

Not needing to change anything

Fear often hides as self-protection, creating walls between us and deeper connection. Today, try softening those walls: speak a truth, share what you've been avoiding, or sit quietly with yourself. Vulnerability can lead to greater understanding.

APPRECIATING THOUGHT

Awareness and thinking

Like dawn and dusk painting the same sky, opposing views can create something beautiful together. Today, notice what happens when you hold space for difference.

Not making anything happen

Have you ever lost yourself in something beautiful – like reading, creating, or walking in nature – and found that time simply melts away? That's flow, a glimpse of life's natural grace.

APPRECIATING THOUGHT

Images

When you feel overwhelmed today, imagine your breath as a caring friend. Let it soothe you, support you, remind you that you're not alone.

PLACE OF NO EFFORT

Not looking forward

Imagine a calm lake, perfectly reflecting the sky above. Just for a moment, see if you can be like that peaceful water – not chasing after things or pushing them away, just letting experiences come and go naturally. What do you notice when you remain this quiet and clear?

Heads and tails

Today's invitation: try to move your body – dance, stretch, walk in nature. Notice how physical movement can shift your mental state. Let your body lead you to joy.

PLACE OF NO EFFORT

Flow belongs to anyone

Have you noticed how sometimes the harder you try to make something happen, the more it slips away? The tighter you squeeze, the less you can hold. Often it's when we finally let go that things naturally fall into place.

A remarkable phenomenon

Give three genuine compliments today. Watch how freely sharing appreciation creates ripples of happiness in your environment.

No need for effort

Pause today to view your life's journey from a wider lens – where you've been, how far you've come, and where you're heading. This broader perspective often reveals growth we've missed in our usual day-to-day focus.

APPRECIATING THOUGHT

Listening

Eat one meal today without devices. Notice colors, textures, flavors. Let eating become a mindfulness practice, a time to nourish body and soul.

PLACE OF NO EFFORT

The field of effortlessness

It is said that "The root of compassion is compassion for oneself." Are there any ways in which you can show yourself kindness and compassion today? Can you thank yourself for the efforts you make, that often go unnoticed?

Radio

Small acts of kindness can create waves of wellbeing – for others and yourself. See if you can sprinkle any into your day. Hold the door, let someone merge in traffic, share a genuine "thank you."

Timelessness

The great teacher Yongey Mingyur Rinpoche once said, "Ultimately, happiness comes down to choosing between the discomfort of becoming aware of your mental afflictions and the discomfort of being ruled by them."

Kinds of thinking

Check in with your body as you read this.
Are you holding tension anywhere? Perhaps
your jaw is clenched? What does it feel like
to gently release it?

Losing linear time

Try setting intentions today for your week ahead. What's something you want to make more room for in your day, your week, your year? Give yourself the space to find some quiet, and listen to your inner voice. We have nothing if we are not intentional with our time.

Breath and thinking

If you interact with someone today, really try to notice them. So often we take small interactions for granted. But by bringing a deeper, gentle attention, we can really change the quality of each interaction.

No clock

Try to practice distance from your emotions when something bothers you. Can you pause before you act, inquire before you respond? Training this part of yourself will help to bring inner peace. As the Dalai Lama says: "With equanimity, you can deal with situations with calm and reason while keeping your inner happiness."

Introduction to deeper mindfulness

Before sleep, name three good things about your day, no matter how small. Our minds naturally dwell on the negatives. Training your mind to spot the positive rewires your brain for happiness.

Free from time

Try to find one similarity between yourself and a stranger today. Realizing we are more connected than what we typically see on the surface is what can bring us together.

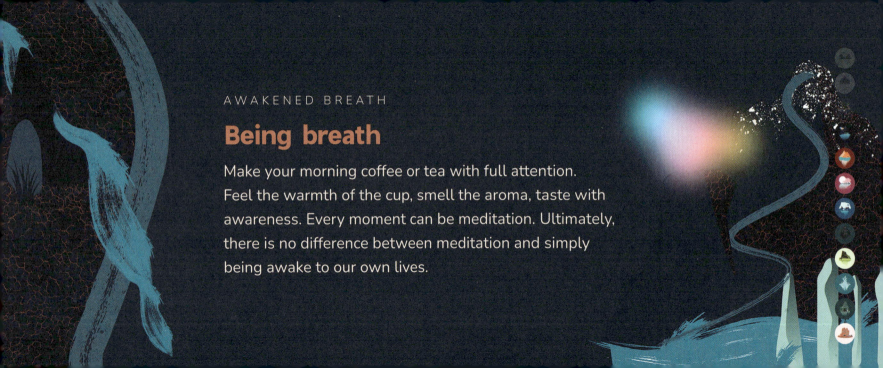

AWAKENED BREATH

Being breath

Make your morning coffee or tea with full attention.
Feel the warmth of the cup, smell the aroma, taste with
awareness. Every moment can be meditation. Ultimately,
there is no difference between meditation and simply
being awake to our own lives.

TIMELESS NOW

Spacious Now

Practice this: Let each breath be complete in itself. Not building to anything, just this breath, then this one.

Just breath (part ii)

Call someone you care about today, just to say hello. Real connection is one of life's greatest sources of happiness. Can you notice any sensations before, during, or after the call? How does it feel?

ALREADY FULFILLED

Already fulfilled

Today's reminder: You don't need to create peace or clarity – they're already here when we stop disturbing the water. You have everything you need within you.

Just breath (part i)

Notice what drains and what energizes you today. Make small choices that preserve your vitality. Sometimes saying "no" is an act of self-kindness.

ALREADY FULFILLED

Appreciating

What if this moment is already complete?
Notice how the breath moves, sounds arise,
thoughts appear – all by themselves,
already perfect.

Breath and me (part ii)

Instead of waiting for happiness, choose it. Today, do three things that reliably bring you joy – listen to your favorite song, take a short walk, call a friend who makes you laugh.

ALREADY FULFILLED

Intrinsic perfection

Today's wisdom: Everything that arises is allowed. Can you meet each moment with this radical acceptance?

Breath and me (part i)

Every moment is a chance to begin again. When you notice you're caught in stress or worry today, take one conscious breath. It's that simple – reset and start fresh.

Just this

Nothing but this moment. This breath. This sound. This sensation. Can you let everything else fall away?

AWAKENED BREATH

Breath but no one breathing

Like a tree growing through concrete, strength often comes from facing obstacles. Today, notice what challenges are helping you grow stronger.

ALREADY FULFILLED

In love with now

Today's practice: Fall in love with the ordinary. The texture of your clothing, the play of light, the taste of water.

Who watches

When stress hits today, pause and take three deep breaths. Feel your hands and feet. Notice what sensations are arising in your chest. This simple reset can shift your entire state. Use it in traffic, before meetings, or anytime you feel overwhelmed.

Levels of Awakening

Awareness is always here and always peaceful. It's the birthright of every human. Meditation can help us uncover our own unclouded and calm awareness.

AWAKENED BREATH

What is breath

Today, share three genuine smiles with strangers. It's not easy. But this small act can change both their energy and yours. Remember: kindness ripples outward.

FIELD OF AWARENESS

Awareness of body

Let your body be your teacher today. Feel its subtle energies, its natural wisdom, its constant dance with life.

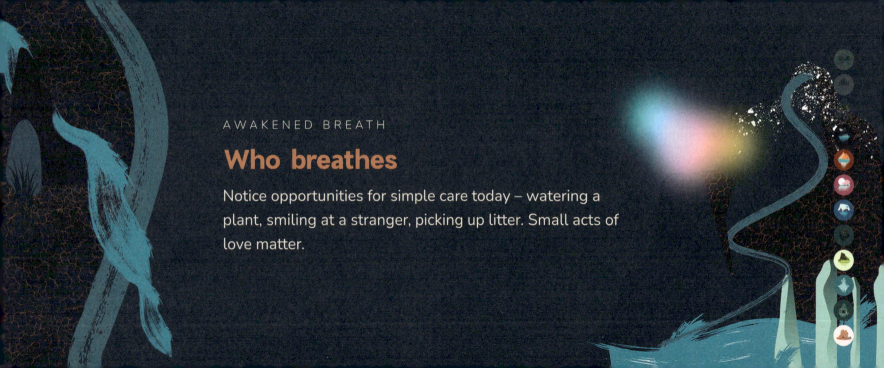

AWAKENED BREATH

Who breathes

Notice opportunities for simple care today – watering a plant, smiling at a stranger, picking up litter. Small acts of love matter.

FIELD OF AWARENESS

Awareness in soundscape

Listen to the spaces between sounds. Notice how awareness holds both sound and silence.

AWAKENED BREATH

What is moving

After every storm, the sun returns. When things feel difficult today, remember: this too shall pass, just like the weather.

Single awareness

The real journey of meditation is a path of change, of growth, of opening up to our experience in any moment and opening our hearts more to this life with all its beauty and its challenges.

Non-dual breath

An old Zen question asks: Who is it breathing? Are you and the sensation of your breath separate, or the same system?

Awakening and the self

Just as every wave is made of ocean, everything in your experience arises from awareness itself. Today, notice the quiet presence that's here before any thought or feeling appears. Can you sense this simple, natural awareness that's always with you?

Absorption (part iii)

Meditation is a homecoming to the stillness that has been waiting for you longer than you can remember.

FIELD OF AWARENESS

All-embracing awareness

Your awareness is like a warm, welcoming room that has space for everything – happy moments, sad feelings, calm times, and stormy thoughts. Nothing needs to be pushed away or changed. Welcome everything that arises with that inviting energy, and notice how your day can change.

BREATH FLOW

Absorption (part ii)

Remember falling in love? How ordinary things suddenly seemed magical? Today, try looking at your life with those fresh eyes again.

Non-dual awareness

Have you noticed how in moments of deep peace, the line between you and what you're experiencing starts to fade? Today, take a moment in nature to allow yourself to rest in these simple moments where everything feels connected and whole.

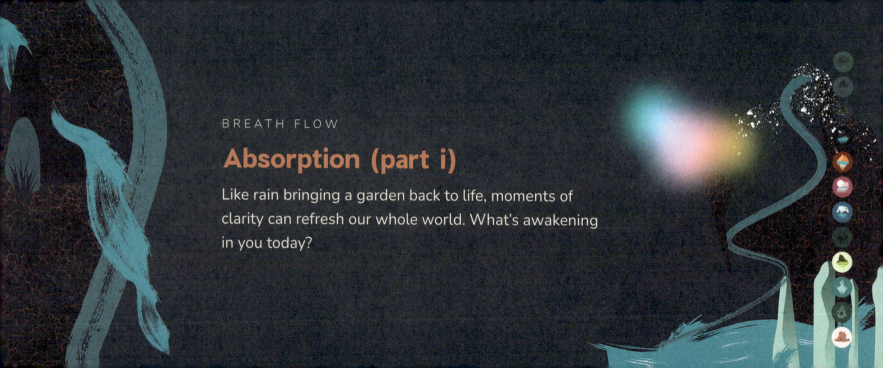

BREATH FLOW

Absorption (part i)

Like rain bringing a garden back to life, moments of clarity can refresh our whole world. What's awakening in you today?

TEMPLE OF IDENTITY

Exploring Self

When you feel happy today, even just a little burst, let yourself really feel it. Like warming your hands by a fire, linger in that warmth for a few extra breaths. The more we do this, the more we wire our brains to feel happiness in the future.

Whole body absorbing

Sometimes we find something that changes everything – like seeing colors for the first time. Today, notice what truly matters to you beneath all the busyness, and see what changes for you.

TEMPLE OF IDENTITY

Exploring name

Every moment is a fresh arising. By being aware of our experience as it occurs, we can come to know, cherish, and appreciate our actual life more deeply.

A deep, dark lake

Try this short exercise. Take a moment, close your eyes, and imagine your mind as a deep, dark lake. Let your experience settle naturally, like sediment sinking to the bottom. Rest here for a breath.

Letting self-image go

"All joy in this world comes from wanting others to be happy, and all suffering in this world comes from wanting only oneself to be happy." — Shantideva

Absorb in breath

Plant a seed of gratitude today – perhaps a heartfelt note to someone on your mind, or words of love to someone dear. Watch how this simple gift blossoms, transforming not just their day, but your own.

Loving the sensation of self

Begin your day by planting a seed of kindness in your heart. Take a quiet moment to imagine how your words and actions might brighten someone's day. Feel the warmth of that intention in your body – this natural glow can guide you toward more caring choices. You might try this simple blessing: "May all beings feel safe, peaceful, and at ease."

Space in breath

Between breaths, there's a moment of perfect quiet. Like the pause between musical notes, these tiny spaces hold their own kind of peace.

TEMPLE OF IDENTITY

Releasing Self

Sometimes the hardest person to be kind to is yourself. Today, try speaking to yourself as you would to a beloved child – with patience, understanding, and care.

Expand-contract (part ii)

Make small moments beautiful today – arrange your breakfast mindfully, take a scenic route, pause to watch clouds. Life is your canvas.

A moment on a beach

Think of someone who showed you kindness in the past. Let that memory warm your heart. Now imagine passing that same kindness forward to others, creating a chain of care that keeps growing. Think of expanding that chain during each of your day's interactions.

Expand-contract (part i)

Feel how your body naturally expands with each breath, like a flower opening to sunlight. Notice the gentle space this creates inside you.

Self as gateway

Like tending a garden, nurture kindness throughout your day – in what you do, what you say, and especially in what you think. Notice the stories playing in your mind and gently guide them toward compassion. The more you practice this, the more natural kindness becomes, like a well-worn path in a meadow.

Unconditional wellbeing

Happiness isn't always about finding something new – it's often about noticing what's already here. Today, pause to feel the simple comfort of being alive. What a gift it is.

TEMPLE OF IDENTITY

Self as seed

"Hate is never conquered by hate. Hate is conquered by love. This is an eternal law."
— The Dhammapada

BREATH SUPPORT

Carried by breath

Often we feel like we need to control our breath. But actually, we don't. In a way, the breath carries us. It nourishes us and keeps us alive – without us needing to do anything.

To be a beginner

If you ever run into a person who causes you frustration or discomfort, remember they too have hopes, fears, and dreams just like you. They too are a beginner, in many respects. How does this shift your perspective?

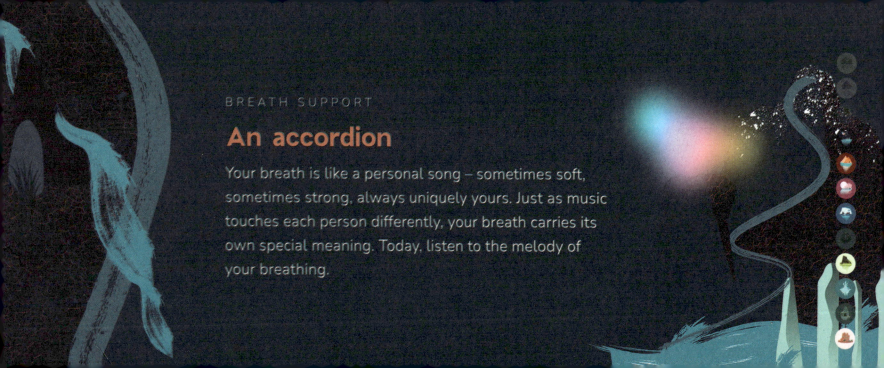

BREATH SUPPORT

An accordion

Your breath is like a personal song – sometimes soft, sometimes strong, always uniquely yours. Just as music touches each person differently, your breath carries its own special meaning. Today, listen to the melody of your breathing.

Not knowing

Sometimes the wisest answer is "I don't know." Today, notice how uncertainty can feel spacious and alive, like standing at the edge of a beautiful vista.

BREATH SUPPORT

A simple room in Santa Fe

Each breath supports us like a trusted friend. It's been with you since birth – it was the very first thing you ever did.

Not understanding

Give yourself a break from figuring everything out. Like watching clouds drift by, let your thoughts move without needing to understand or solve them.

Breath connection

While walking today – to your car, through the office, in your home – feel your feet on the ground. Notice the sensations of heel and toes. This simple noticing is enough to connect us to the present moment.

The compass bearing

Happiness isn't always about changing things – sometimes it's about discovering the peace that's already here. Today, pause occasionally and feel the simple joy of being alive.

Shared breath

Give yourself five deep, slow breaths. Try to do it without reading, or being distracted by your mobile phone. Eyes closed or gently lowered. Notice how this small boundary creates a little more spaciousness in your experience.

Not judging

Your breath has been with you since your first moment. Right now, feel its gentle movement. No need to change or judge it – just let it remind you that you're here, alive and breathing. Isn't it a comfort to know that it has been with you all along?

Receiving breath

Each breath is both a giving and receiving – you share this air with trees, birds, and every living thing. Feel how this simple act connects you to all of life.

The new now

Each moment is fresh, like morning dew on grass. Today, try looking at familiar things as if seeing them for the first time – your hands, the sky, the faces of those you love.

BREATH SUPPORT

Enjoying breath as support

Nature thrives on partnership – flowers need both sun and rain, soil needs both rest and disturbance. What seemingly opposite forces are helping you support you, but are perhaps going unnoticed?

UNDERSTANDING OURSELVES

A moment of rest

By coming back to the present moment, we are
allowing ourselves to rest our nervous systems
and to appreciate the very fact of being alive.

MINDFUL BREATHING

Mindfulness breathes

Just for a moment, on your next breath in, can you notice how it feels? Practice receiving each breath today as a gift. No need to control or change anything. Simply accept what's being offered in each moment.

Who sees and hears?

Next time you hear birds singing or feel sunshine on your skin, pause for a moment. Just listen, just feel. Notice how peaceful it is to simply be present with these everyday moments.

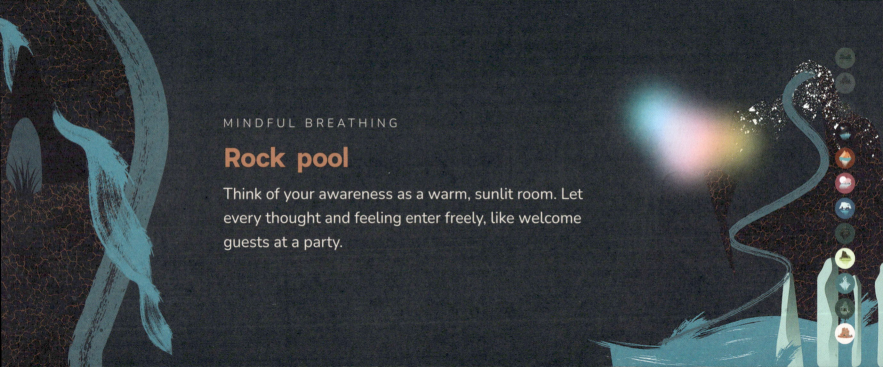

MINDFUL BREATHING

Rock pool

Think of your awareness as a warm, sunlit room. Let every thought and feeling enter freely, like welcome guests at a party.

Whose body?

Your body is a miracle of life – breathing, moving, sensing all by itself. Today, appreciate this amazing gift that connects you to the whole living world.

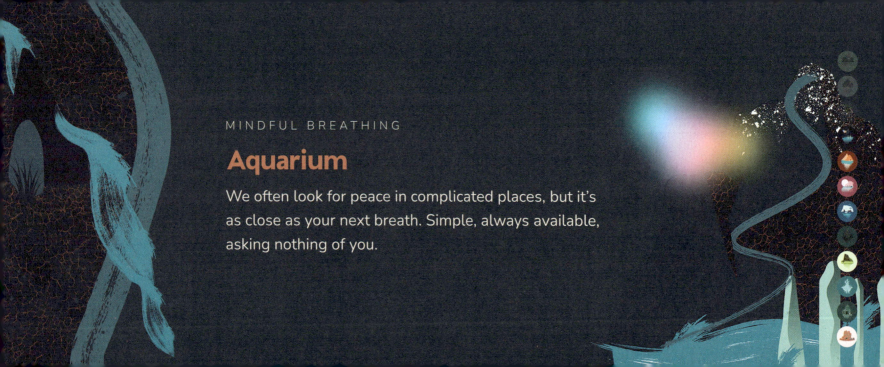

MINDFUL BREATHING

Aquarium

We often look for peace in complicated places, but it's as close as your next breath. Simple, always available, asking nothing of you.

Who breathes?

Take a deep breath. Now let it out completely.
Notice how the next breath comes all by itself,
like waves returning to shore. Life breathes you.

MINDFUL BREATHING

Ocean waves

Your heart knows how to beat, your lungs know how to breathe. Isn't it wonderful? These systems are here for you, giving you life. Today, notice how they are working alongside you through everything you do. You are a part of this natural beauty.

Awakening in the margins

The most profound moments often come when we least expect them – waiting in line, washing dishes, walking to the car. Can you find the hidden beauty in an ordinary moment today?

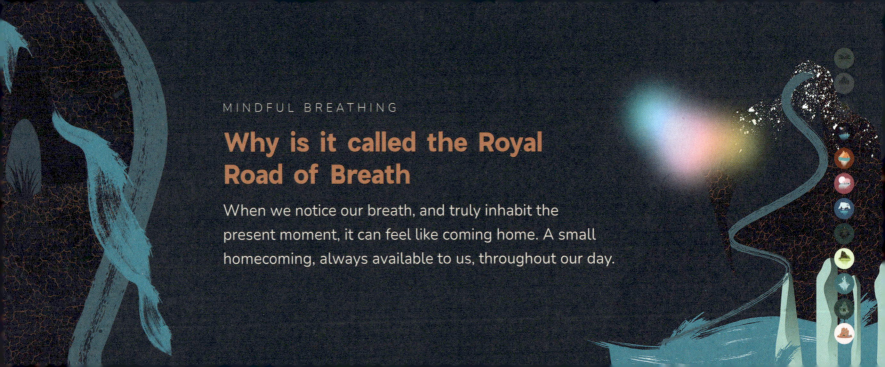

MINDFUL BREATHING

Why is it called the Royal Road of Breath

When we notice our breath, and truly inhabit the present moment, it can feel like coming home. A small homecoming, always available to us, throughout our day.

Whose experience?

The body lives in the present, but the mind is a time traveler. It likes to rehash past events and rehearse future events. Pay attention while the mind tries to do this today, can you stop the imagination and come back to the present moment?

Six point breath

Each breath is a reminder that life is happening now. The past is gone, the future is uncertain, but this breath—this very moment—is real and alive.

Ordinary mind

Your thoughts are like clouds passing through the sky – some dark, some light, all temporary. Today, just watch them float by without trying to change them.

Sunlit cloth

Each inhale and exhale is a reminder of the impermanence of all things. Just as the breath arises and passes away, so do thoughts, feelings, and experiences. Embracing this rhythm, we learn to let go and flow with the ever-changing nature of life.

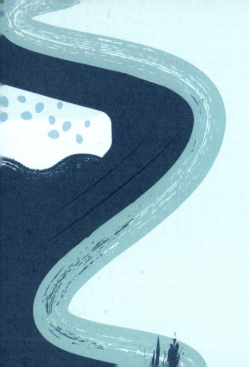

Introduction to aspects of being

You have a natural, built-in capacity for peace, even amongst a busy and difficult life. Today, try and take one moment to notice that you are alive. You are simply being, without the need for doing.

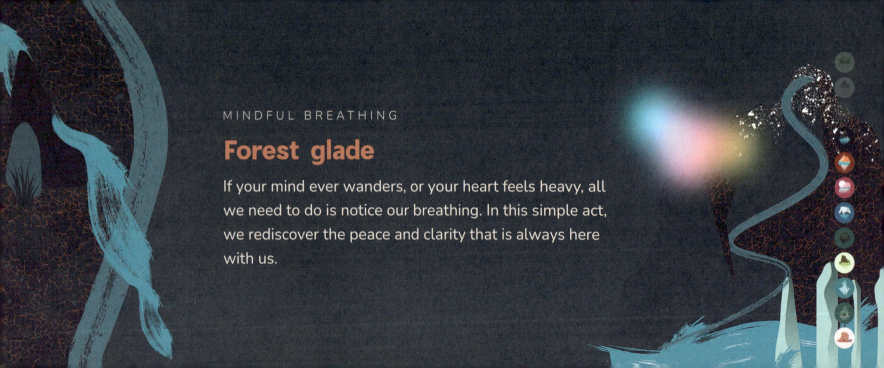

MINDFUL BREATHING

Forest glade

If your mind ever wanders, or your heart feels heavy, all we need to do is notice our breathing. In this simple act, we rediscover the peace and clarity that is always here with us.

Listening for the mind

Thoughts can be like radio stations playing in your mind. Right now, just for a moment, practice being the listener. What can you hear playing?

MINDFUL BREATHING

Introduction to Royal Road of Breath

In meditation, the breath is known as "The Royal Road". Because it's always here, always available to bring us back to the present. All we need to do is notice it, and we're already back in presence. Over the coming days, we'll explore the breath together more deeply.

SILENCE

Sounds of the world

The world is alive with sound – distant traffic,
rustling leaves, humming machines. Let these
sounds come to you without naming or judging
them – just letting them be.

Letting go

Like waves shifting sand, each breath
naturally cleanses and refreshes. No need
to control it – just watch what changes,
disappears, and settles.

Field of silence

It's not the things we do in life, but the very experience of being alive, being conscious, that is the real gift. And meditation is an exercise that helps us unwrap it and receive it.

One bright pearl (part ii)

Notice how your breath changes with your mood – quick with excitement, slow with peace. Let it be your teacher today about what you're really feeling.

Breathing silence

Each breath has a natural pause at its end – a moment of perfect stillness. Today, notice these tiny islands of peace in your everyday breathing.

One bright pearl (part i)

You carry a bright pearl within – your true nature. Today, let its light shine through everything you do. Every moment is an opportunity to polish this gem.

SILENCE

Receiving silence

Sometimes the greatest gift we can give ourselves is a moment of quiet. Let silence be your companion today, refreshing your spirit.

JOURNEY INTO THE UNKNOWN

This too

Whatever arises, add "this too." This too is welcome. This too can be held. This too is part of the journey. Let this phrase open your heart today.

Becoming silence

As the great teacher Jon Kabat-Zinn says, "Physiologically, as long as we are breathing, there is more right with us than wrong."

Speedy's dog

Like looking for your reflection in a foggy mirror, seeking the self can be tricky, because it's too close to see. Today, rather than searching, simply pause and ask: "What is it that's aware right now? What knows these thoughts, these sensations, this breathing?"

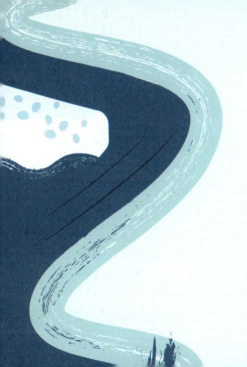

STILLNESS

What is being?

You don't have to earn the right to exist. Like flowers naturally blooming, your being here is already complete.

Pass the jug

What you receive, pass along. Today, notice opportunities to share kindness – a smile given freely, a moment of patience, a small act of help. Watch how easily kindness grows and ripples outward. One simple gesture can touch many lives, creating waves of goodwill in the world around us.

Tracking momentum

Life can feel like a rushing river. Today, try one time to notice when you're caught in the current of doing, and give yourself permission to step onto the bank and rest.

99 curves

The path of life rarely goes straight. We are always beset by twists and turns. Can you trust that these twists and turns are in fact there to teach us, to challenge us, and to help us grow?

Stillness in the body

Your body knows how to find stillness, like a tree settling after wind. As you read this, take a small moment to be still, and let yourself be quietly rooted.

Oak tree

Often, in the midst of a busy day, all we need is a brief moment of rest. Resting our body, resting our nervous system, resting our mind. See if you can find a short moment to grant yourself some rest today.

Stillness in the mind

Just behind all your thoughts is a vast, peaceful space of awareness – like the deep blue sky behind clouds. Always there, always waiting for you. Can you step into it?

Rice in the bowl

What will give you energy today? Maybe it's a quiet cup of coffee, a friend's smile, or a moment of rest. These simple pleasures can be the most nourishing for the heart.

Stillness in the heart

If your heart is troubled, take a moment to imagine it being held in gentle hands. Try to treat your emotions with the same kindness you'd offer a dear friend, and you may find the burden ease.

JOURNEY INTO THE UNKNOWN

The next moment is unknown

Today, like every day, will offer you a mix of experiences — some welcome, some not. Can you receive these experiences with curiosity, rather than judgement? What's being offered right now?

Stillness and obstacles

Sometimes life's obstacles turn out to be guides. Can you look at one of life's difficult challenges with fresh eyes? Could there be something valuable to learn, waiting within the challenge?

ORIGINAL FACE

Original Nature

Like the sky containing all weather, your original nature includes everything. Today, let all experiences come and go while resting in your fundamental openness.

STILLNESS

Breath and stillness

Each breath is like a door opening to peace. Today, let your breathing remind you that stillness is always available, right here within you.

Warm or cold

Is this moment warm or cold? Not the temperature, but the feeling tone of experience itself. Today, notice the natural warmth of awareness that holds everything.

A larger stillness

If you're ever feeling alone, remember: you're actually part of something so large and beautiful. You're deeply connected to the world around you, to life on earth.

ORIGINAL FACE

Original face

Who were you before you could talk? Can you remember that childlike innocence? Today, try looking beneath your social identity to something more essential. It's always been here, waiting to be recognized.

STILLNESS

Dissolving into stillness

Rain doesn't try to fall, it simply falls. See if you can find a moment to naturally settle into your experience, without forcing or striving.

ORIGINAL FACE

Unmoveable bowl

When you catch yourself rushing today, take a breath and ask: "What really matters right now?" Be curious about your answer, and remember to enjoy the journey that each moment brings.

Two kinds of presence

Sometimes we create presence by paying attention. Sometimes presence finds us, like sunshine breaking through clouds.

ORIGINAL FACE

Winds of life

Like a tree with deep roots, you can bend
with life's winds while staying grounded.
Today, feel this natural strength within you.

Presence as witness

You are the quiet awareness that watches your life unfold. Like a movie screen that shows many different scenes, you remain unchanged by what appears and disappears.

ORIGINAL FACE

3 knocks, 3 shakes

Listen for three different sounds right now – maybe distant, middle, and close. Notice how each one touches you differently. This simple practice can bring you back to the present moment.

Present with breath

Each breath is brand new, never to be repeated. Just now, as you read these words, let your breathing anchor you to this new moment, always beginning again. How lucky we are, that every moment is a fresh start!

ORIGINAL FACE

No mirror

Like stepping back to see a whole starlit sky instead of just a few stars, try taking a wider view of yourself today. You might be surprised by how much beauty you discover when you look at your whole story instead of just today's chapter.

PRESENCE

Body in presence

Your body is always in the now. Whenever you become lost in thought, just come back to these simple sensations – feet on the ground, hands touching, heart beating.

Polishing the mirror

Your true nature reflects everything, like a clear mirror. Today, notice how awareness naturally shows whatever appears – thoughts, feelings, sensations – while remaining unchanged itself.

Choosing presence

Life's richness reveals itself when we show up for it. Today, take the time to be really present for a simple moment – a sip of water, a friend's voice, a gentle breeze. What do these things feel like when we notice them fully?

ORIGINAL FACE

Nowhere

Where does your mind actually reside?
Can you notice that awareness has no
location? It seems to be everywhere and
yet nowhere.

PRESENCE

First snow

When you eat today, take just a moment to appreciate all the hands that helped bring food to your plate – the farmers, drivers, cooks, and countless others. This simple gratitude makes each meal more meaningful.

ORIGINAL FACE

Introduction to original face

Before thoughts arise, before words form –
what's here? Can you catch a glimpse of
your essential nature, the one that's been
here all along, before any story about
yourself began?

Qualities of presence

As the teacher Tenzin Priyadarshi said, "If there is no stillness, there is no silence. If there is no silence, there is no insight. If there is no insight, there is no clarity."

Sweeping the yard

As you go about your day – sweeping, washing, working – let each task be complete in itself. Nothing extra needed. Everything is already perfect in its ordinariness.

PRESENCE

Kindness of presence

Instead of searching for happiness, try noticing what's already here. Like opening your curtains to find sunshine – it was always there, just waiting to be seen.

Separateness and non-separateness

The tea and the drinker, the sight and the seer – are they really separate? Today, notice moments when the usual boundaries between self and experience soften naturally.

PRESENCE

Restful and aware

Our one true quest is to know ourselves ever more deeply. To fall in love with who and what we are, to let that love shine in the world just the way it needs to.

Moving like bamboo

Like bamboo bending in the wind, true strength is flexible. Today, notice where you can bend rather than break. What happens when you move with life rather than against it?

AWARENESS

Awareness as a facet of being

Today, practice letting things be exactly as they are. Notice how much easier life feels when you don't try to fix or change every moment.

Experience flows

Watch how experience moves like a stream today. Each moment flowing into the next. No need to hold on, just rest in the flow. This is the natural way of things.

Awareness of breath

Take a few slow breaths. Notice how breathing naturally connects you to the world around you – fresh air flowing in, used air flowing out.

WHOLE EARTH

Whole earth support

Whatever arises today, feel the earth
supporting you. Like a mountain unmoved
by changing weather, you're held in every
moment. Let this ground be your refuge.

Awareness breathing

Sometimes we get caught trying to grasp moments of peace. Instead, try letting peace find you. Just be still, and notice what it's like to feel the stillness.

WHOLE EARTH

Mindful medicine

Your body carries ancient wisdom. Today,
notice what brings ease to your system.
A deep breath, a moment of stillness,
the warmth of sunlight. Let these simple
medicines support you.

Awareness seeing

Each morning is a fresh start. Take a quiet moment to begin your day with a simple wish: "May I be gentle with myself and others today."

The whole earth is medicine

Feel the ground beneath your feet today.
You're held by a living planet, connected
to all of life. Can you sense the giant,
supportive presence of the earth beneath you?

Awareness hearing

Today, whenever you feel tense or stuck, imagine opening your hands and letting go. Feel how freedom comes not from getting something new, but from releasing what you're holding.

PILGRIMAGE

Closer than close

What's nearer than your next thought?
Today, notice the awareness that's already
here before you look for it. It's closer than
your breath, more intimate than
any sensation.

Inner and outer awareness

Look around your room right now. Notice something beautiful you usually overlook – maybe sunshine on a wall or the pattern of your coffee mug. Take a moment to really see it.

Who hears

Today, practice saying "I don't know" with wonder rather than worry. Not-knowing is an intimate friend, closer than any concept or belief. What opens up when you release the need to understand? How exciting it is that we still have so much to learn and discover.

Awareness as body

Start small: pick one daily task – like washing dishes or checking email – and bring a touch of patience and kindness to it. Notice how this tiny shift feels.

PILGRIMAGE

Not knowing is most intimate

What is this life? What really is this life that we are granted? Where did it come from? What is it made of? See if you can practice letting yourself be genuinely curious about your experience, throughout your day.

AWARENESS

Loving awareness

Notice when you're being hard on yourself. Take a breath and soften – like turning down a loud radio to find the peaceful music beneath.

The river of consciousness

Notice how nature never rushes — flowers open at their own pace, rivers find their own path. Today, give yourself permission to move at your own natural speed.

AWARENESS

Size of awareness

How big is your awareness? Right now, what is the limit of your awareness? Or, like the sky, does it have no edges?

Where are you going

Like a leaf in the wind, let yourself be carried by life today. Notice the difference between forcing things and allowing them to unfold. Where can you release control?

Space

When talking with someone today, try giving them your full, kind attention – like sunshine that simply warms whatever it touches. Notice how this feels.

PILGRIMAGE

Let the wind carry you

Sometimes healing comes not from doing more, but from doing less. Like a murky pond settling on its own, let yourself be still and see what comes through the surface.

Space and breath

Your body is lighter than you think. Feel this natural ease as you walk, stretch, or simply sit quietly.

The gateless gate

Life itself is wild and unknowable. Today, instead of seeking answers, rest in the questions. Let yourself be puzzled, surprised, delighted. Life is full of things we don't know.

SPACE

Space in soundscape

As you move through your day, imagine gliding easily like a leaf on water. Let this feeling of grace stay with you.

Life's journey is unknown

As you move through your day, imagine everyone you meet wishes for happiness, just as you do. This shared humanity connects us all. Let this understanding soften any barriers in your heart.

SPACE

Space in body

Listen to the sounds around you right now –
maybe birds, voices, or distant traffic. Notice the
peaceful moments between these sounds.

Universal kindness

If resistance arises today, try softening around it. What happens when you allow discomfort to be part of your wholeness? Sometimes the path to peace isn't getting what we want, but embracing what is already here.

The player and the percussion

Sometimes it feels as if life plays you like an instrument, each experience creating a unique note. You are the musician, but you can also listen to the music. Can you let yourself resonate with whatever arises?

Wider well-wishing

Today's practice: wherever you go, silently wish everyone well. The cashier, the stranger on the street, the difficult colleague. Notice how this simple practice changes your experience of the day.

Body in space

Notice how your breath naturally finds its own rhythm, like waves finding the shore. No effort needed – just let it flow.

A friend or relative

Think of someone you care about. Let their face come to mind. Send them silent wishes for wellbeing. Notice how this natural care lives in your heart. Today, let this feeling of connection guide your actions.

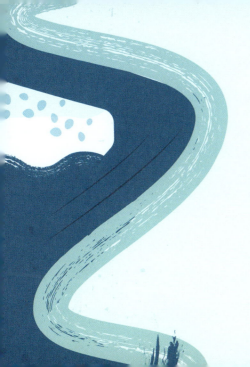

SPACE

Outer experience as space

Sometimes it feels like the world isn't solid – it's more like a dance of light and energy in space. Can you notice how everything emerges from and returns to openness?

Compassion as a feeling

Compassion has a texture – warm, tender, spacious. Today, notice moments when your heart naturally opens to others' experiences. These aren't moments to create, but to recognize and allow.

Inner experience as space

When something pulls at you today, try this gentle practice: First, just pause. Take a quiet breath. That's enough to begin. Next, notice what you're feeling in your body – any tension or urges. Just observe them, like watching clouds pass by. Then, give yourself permission to be exactly as you are right now.

LOVING AWARENESS

An older loved one

Remember an older loved one who touched your life. Their hopes for your happiness, their belief in you. Carry this loving presence with you today. Let it remind you that you're part of a larger story of caring for each other.

Why we go back to basics

Like trees sharing nutrients through underground networks, we're all connected in invisible ways. Can you think: what ways are you connected to people in your life?

LOVING AWARENESS

A mentor

Bring to mind someone who has shown you
true kindness. Feel their presence with you.
If self-doubt creeps in, you can ask: "What
would they say to me right now?"

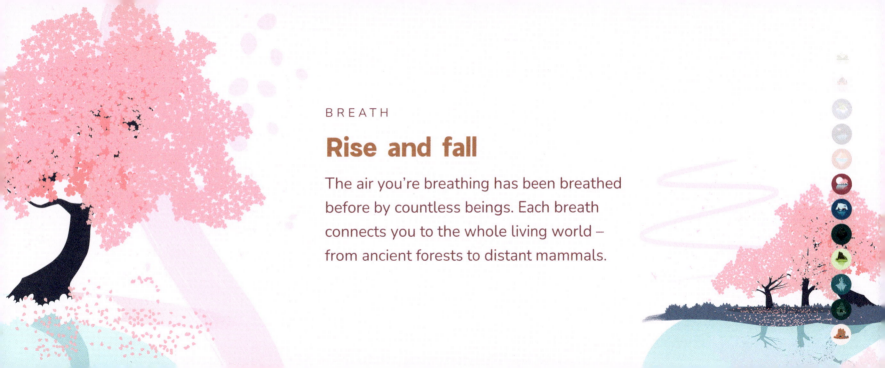

BREATH

Rise and fall

The air you're breathing has been breathed before by countless beings. Each breath connects you to the whole living world – from ancient forests to distant mammals.

Self kindness (part ii)

Today, whenever something difficult arises, pause and ask: "What would self-kindness look like in this moment?" Sometimes it's taking a breath. Sometimes it's setting a boundary. Always, it's making room for the fact that we are humans who deserve love.

BREATH

Breath at the nostrils

Sometimes the deepest wisdom comes from the simplest things. Today, try to return to the basics – feel your breath, notice your steps, taste your food. Everything you need for happiness is right here.

Self kindness (part i)

Notice the voice you use with yourself today. Would you speak to a dear friend this way? Try treating yourself with the same understanding you'd offer someone you love. You're carrying so much – let kindness be your ground.

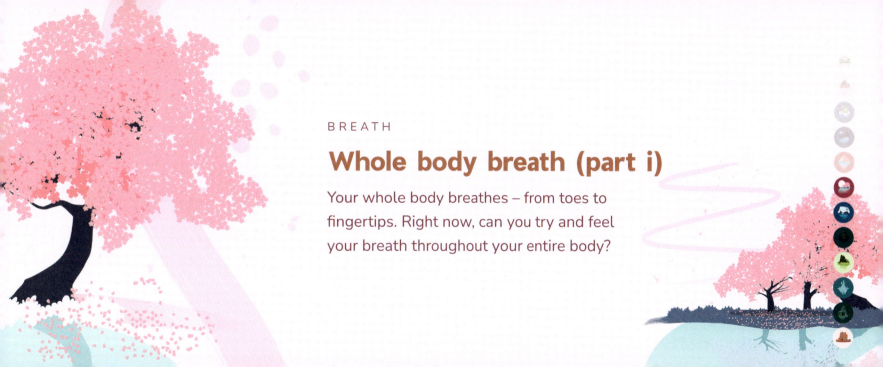

BREATH

Whole body breath (part i)

Your whole body breathes – from toes to fingertips. Right now, can you try and feel your breath throughout your entire body?

Kindness intro

Begin today by placing a hand on your heart. Feel its steady rhythm. This simple gesture can remind you that kindness starts right here, with this basic warmth toward your own experience. What would change if you moved through today with this gentle hand of friendship on your heart?

Whole body breath (part ii)

Approach your everyday experience with gentleness. Let your attention be soft, patient, and kind. Give this love to yourself and others.

No ulterior motive

A garden teaches patience – seeds need time, plants grow at their own pace. What's growing slowly but surely in your life right now?

The shy mare

Your heart knows things your mind can't figure out. Today, listen to its quiet wisdom – it speaks in feelings, in moments of pause and silence.

EXPLORING PREFERENCE

Absence of preference

When you read this, take three conscious breaths. Feel the simple miracle of being alive. Before plans and desires fill your mind, rest in this basic awareness that needs nothing added.

Expansion and contraction

When was the last time you smiled at a stranger? All humans share the same system of emotions, the same type of conscious mind. In this way, we are already connected with any stranger we meet.

Dislike and whole

You are already complete. Today's invitation: whenever you notice yourself wanting something to be different, pause and feel the wholeness that's already here. Your basic nature includes everything – both the wanting and the peace.

Peace-bringing breath

Like a flower naturally turning toward light, there's an innate goodness in you. Today, trust this basic wisdom that knows how to grow toward what's true.

EXPLORING PREFERENCE

Wanting and whole

Your mind can be like the ocean — waves on the surface, but calm in the depths. When surface thoughts are choppy, remember your deeper quiet.

Becoming breath (part i)

We don't have to think about our next breath, it just comes, because it is. Be like your breath – effortless, steadfast, and everlasting.

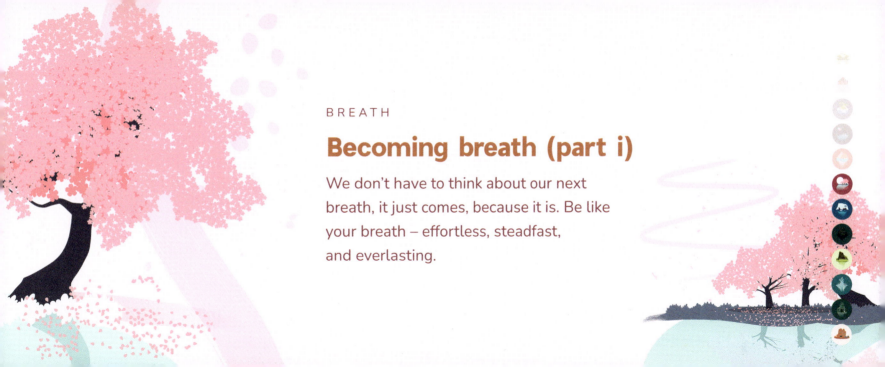

Drying coffee pots on retreat

Everyone has creativity within them. It might show up in cooking, problem-solving, arranging flowers, or choosing words. How will you express yours today?

BREATH

Becoming breath (part ii)

Your breath connects you to the world and universe around you. The trees, your neighbors, a butterfly, and a friend. We all take in the same air, and share the beauty of this innate experience of being.

Unpleasant and aversion

Life pulses between effort and rest, solitude and connection, speaking and silence. Today, notice how these natural rhythms move through your hours.

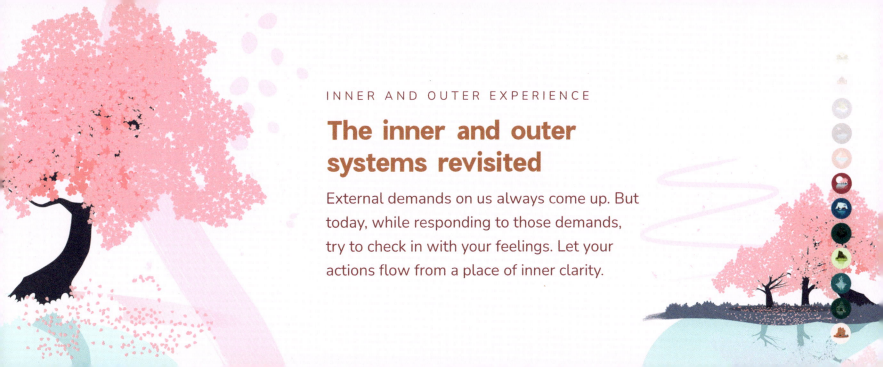

The inner and outer systems revisited

External demands on us always come up. But today, while responding to those demands, try to check in with your feelings. Let your actions flow from a place of inner clarity.

EXPLORING PREFERENCE

Unpleasant

Look up at the stars tonight. Like lights scattered across velvet, they remind us that beauty often emerges from darkness.

Outer channels (part i)

The world offers constant gifts – birdsong, warm sunlight, fresh air. Today, pause occasionally to receive these simple treasures that surround you.

Pleasant and wanting

Watch leaves falling from trees. They don't struggle or cling – they simply release when it's time. What could you gently let go of today?

Outer channels (part ii)

Happiness often comes from the smallest things. Today, smile at a friend, feel the sunlight on your face, watch the rain fall. The smallest smile can change the world. Change your world today.

Pleasant

Joy often lives in small moments – a sweet animal, a comfortable chair, a friend's smile. Today, don't let these gifts pass you by without noticing them.

Inner channels: talk + image

Your inner dialogue shapes your day. Notice if you're being harsh with yourself. Can you speak to yourself as you would to a friend?

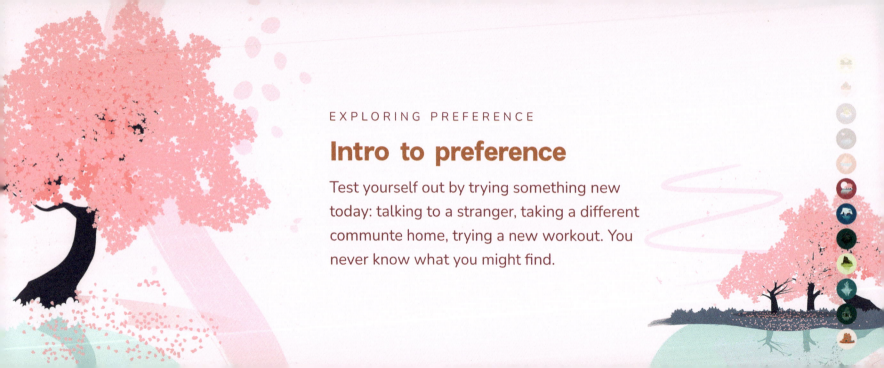

EXPLORING PREFERENCE

Intro to preference

Test yourself out by trying something new today: talking to a stranger, taking a different commute home, trying a new workout. You never know what you might find.

Inner channels: torso

Your heart carries deep knowing. Before making decisions, check in with your feelings. Sometimes emotional wisdom is clearer than logic.

INNER AND OUTER EXPERIENCE

Whole and gone

We all have likes and dislikes. Today, notice what you resist and what you chase. Could some peace come from accepting things as they are?

The fabric of memories

Memories can transport us instantly. Today, notice when past moments surface. Neither chase nor push them away – just watch them and let them flow through your mind.

INNER AND OUTER EXPERIENCE

Whole

We can often feel like something is missing. Like we're striving towards a thing we need to get to. For today, trying experimenting with the idea that this moment — exactly as it is — could be enough.